OUR WORLD
OUR FUTURE

Saving
Water

Sharon Dalgleish

CHELSEA HOUSE
PUBLISHERS
A Haights Cross Communications Company
Philadelphia

This edition first published in 2003 in the United States of America by Chelsea House Publishers, a subsidiary of Haights Cross Communications.

Chelsea House Publishers
1974 Sproul Road, Suite 400
Broomall, PA 19008-0914

The Chelsea House world wide web address is www.chelseahouse.com

Library of Congress Cataloging-in-Publication Data

Dalgleish, Sharon.
    Saving water / by Sharon Dalgleish.

        v. cm. — (Our world: our future)

    Contents: Our world—Our future—Weird water—Living in a watery world—Water and weather—Storing water—Using water at home—Waste water down the drain—Water for factories—Thirsty cows and crops—From drains to waterways—Dissolving-good and bad—Project water—Think globally—Sustaining our world.

    ISBN 0-7910-7016-6

    1. Water-supply—Juvenile literature. 2. Water conservation—Juvenile literature.
    [1. Water. 2. Water conservation.] I. Title. II. Our world: our future (Philadelphia, Pa.)

    TD348 .D25 2003

    363.6'1—dc21

                                                            2002002522

First published in 2002 by
MACMILLAN EDUCATION AUSTRALIA PTY LTD
627 Chapel Street, South Yarra, Australia, 3141

Edited by Sally Woollett
Text design by Karen Young
Cover design by Karen Young
Page layout and simple diagrams by Nina Sanadze
Technical illustrations and maps by Pat Kermode, Purple Rabbit Productions

Printed in China

Acknowledgements
Cover photograph: Michaelmas Cay, Queensland, courtesy of Coo-ee Picture Library.

AAP/AFP Photo/Chris Wilkins, p. 22 (bottom); ANT Photo Library, p. 11 (bottom); Australian Picture Library/Corbis, p. 24 (bottom); Coo-ee Picture Library, pp. 12 (left), 14, 15 (right), 23 (top and bottom), 27 (left); The DW Stock Picture Library, pp. 4 (top left, top center, top right and bottom left), 11 (top), 17 (top), 20 (top); Victor Englebert, pp. 9 (top), 15 (left), 19, 21; Getty/FPG International, p. 7; Getty Images/Image Bank, p. 28; Getty Images/Photodisc, pp. 4 (bottom center), 8 (top), 30; Great Southern Stock, pp. 6 (top right), 17 (bottom); Imageaddict.com, p. 4 (bottom right); Fred Adler/Kino Archives, pp. 13 (top), 18 (left and right), 22 (top); Legend Images, pp. 6 (top left and bottom), 9 (bottom); Wade Hughes/Lochman Transparencies, p. 20 (bottom); Dr Stuart Miller/Lochman Transparencies, p. 8 (bottom); NASA, p. 10; Brian Parker, p. 12 (right); Dale Mann/Retrospect, p. 16; Southern Images/Silkstone, pp. 13 (bottom), 27 (right); Mark Edwards/Still Pictures, p. 29; World Images, p. 24 (top).

Contents

READ
MORE ABOUT:

Look out for this box. It will tell you the other pages in this book where you can find out more about related topics.

Our world

We are connected to everything in our world. We are connected through the air we breathe, the water we drink, the food we eat, the energy we use, and the soil we live on.

To keep our world healthy, all these elements must work together.

water

land

energy

wildlife

forests

air

SHOW ME

The parts of your body work together to keep you healthy. If one part of your body stops working properly, you get sick!

4

Our future

The number of people in our world is now doubling every 40 years. This means that when you are grown up there could be twice as many people on Earth as there are now.

Every person on Earth needs certain things to survive. We need to make sure our world will still be able to give people everything they need to live, now and in the future.

▲ Now.

▲ Forty years from now.

STOP & THINK

Suppose that one part of our world were to stop working properly. What do you think might happen to the rest of our world?

5

Weird water

▲ Does ice flow? What shape is ice?

Water is a liquid. It moves and flows. It will take on the shape of anything you pour it into. But water is special. It is more than just an ordinary liquid. It can easily change to a solid or a gas.

When water is cooled, it freezes and becomes ice. Ice is a solid.

When water is warmed up, it changes into water vapor. That is why wet laundry dries when you hang it out. The water **evaporates** into the air. Water vapor is a gas.

Think about wood. It cannot change from a solid to a liquid to a gas under ordinary conditions on Earth. No other substance can either. Water is the only one that can easily perform this magic act and change into all three!

SHOW ME

Pour a glass of water. What shape is the water? Pour the glass of water into another container. What shape is the water now?

◄ When a kettle boils, the liquid water turns to steam. Steam is water vapor, an invisible gas. The part of steam you can see is actually tiny droplets of liquid water in the air.

Wonderful water

It is important that water can change its form so easily. We need water, water vapor and ice to live. They are all part of an amazing recycling act called the water cycle.

Water from rivers and oceans, on the ground, in puddles and on plants is heated by the sun. This heat changes the water to water vapor. The vapor rises into the air. In the air, the water vapor cools and forms clouds. It then turns back into liquid drops of water. When the drops get too big and heavy, they fall as rain and fill up the oceans and rivers. Then the whole cycle starts again.

▲ Even your sweat evaporates and joins the water cycle!

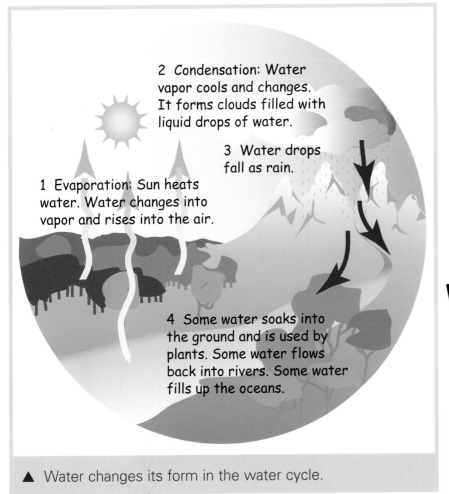

2 Condensation: Water vapor cools and changes. It forms clouds filled with liquid drops of water.

3 Water drops fall as rain.

1 Evaporation: Sun heats water. Water changes into vapor and rises into the air.

4 Some water soaks into the ground and is used by plants. Some water flows back into rivers. Some water fills up the oceans.

▲ Water changes its form in the water cycle.

STOP & THINK
The water cycle keeps water always on the move. What would happen if the water cycle stopped?

OUR FUTURE

Living in a watery world

Water is everywhere in our world. Fog and clouds are made of it. The air we breathe has water in it. Even your own body is mostly water. You are about 70 percent water, with just enough solid material to hold you together!

Earth is mostly water, too. Water covers about 70 percent of Earth's surface. Most of this water—97 percent—is salty water in oceans and seas. Have you ever been to the beach and swallowed a mouthful of water? It tastes awful because it is salty.

▲ From space Earth looks very blue. The large blue areas in this photo are the Atlantic and Indian Oceans. The white patches are clouds. Clouds are made of water, too! The pink and orange areas are land.

▲ Much of Earth's fresh water is frozen in glaciers.

STOP & THINK

If there is such a small amount of fresh water, why has it never run out?

To survive, people need to drink fresh, unsalty water. Fresh water is water that falls as rain or snow. Most of this fresh water is deep underground or frozen in **glaciers**. This leaves only a tiny amount of fresh water for people, and most animals and plants, to get at and use.

Using fresh water

So far we have not run out of fresh water because we can use the same small amount over and over again. Our world recycles it for us in the water cycle.

The problem is, as our population grows we use more and more water.

- We use water for cooking and cleaning.
- We flush water down the toilet.
- We use water to grow our food.
- We use water when we make things in factories.
- We store water to use later.

In a rainforest, the whole water cycle happens in one day. Rainforests are an important part of the water cycle, but we are cutting them down.

We can survive days, sometimes even months, without food. We cannot survive more than a few days without water. The amount of drinkable water in the water cycle is not endless, and we need to make sure that it does not run out.

▲ The mist above this rainforest in Colombia is made from water that has evaporated from the trees.

SHOW ME

Fill a bucket with water. Imagine that this is all the water in our world. Now fill a teacup with water from the bucket. This would be all the fresh water in our world.

Now take a teaspoonful of water from the cup. This teaspoonful of water is the only fresh water we can reach and use.

water in our world   fresh water in our world   fresh water we can reach and use

READ MORE ABOUT:

- using water at home on page 14
- using water in factories on page 18
- using water on farms on page 20.

Water and weather

We cannot drink the salty water in the oceans, but seawater still does a very important job. The water in oceans helps to control the weather in our world. The oceans soak up a lot of heat from the sun in summer. When the weather gets cooler, the water slowly lets this heat go into the air. This stops our world from getting too cold in the winter. The water also soaks up and stores heat in very hot parts of the world and then flows in the oceans to colder places, making them warmer.

Many scientists believe the **greenhouse effect** is causing global warming. Our world—including our oceans—is getting warmer.

Pollution in the **atmosphere** acts like a sheet of glass on a greenhouse. It lets the sunlight through but does not let all the heat back out. Different types of pollution cause this greenhouse effect. These pollutants are sometimes called greenhouse gases.

▲ This is a photograph, taken from the air, of a warm ocean current called the Gulf Stream. Britain's weather would be very cold and icy without it.

STOP & THINK

If you like swimming in warm water, why does it matter if the oceans get warmer?

▶ Greenhouse gases act like the glass of a greenhouse. Large amounts of these gases come from cars, factories, power plants and burning forests.

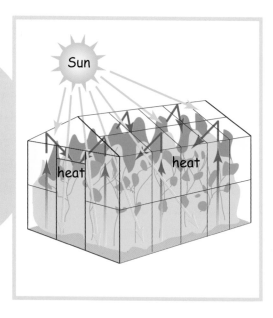

Sun

heat   heat

Water on the rise

Global warming does not mean more sunshine! Warmer oceans cause more evaporation to happen in the water cycle. This means changes to rainfall patterns around our world. Some places will get more rain, other places will get less rain—even drought.

Global warming also means that sea levels will rise, because warmer water takes up more space. As the sea level rises, coastlines and low-lying land will disappear underwater. People living in these areas may have to move away, and some farmland will no longer be available.

Sea ice is important because it reflects heat from the sun back into space. When the ice melts, less heat is reflected. So our world heats up even more!

▲ This sunflower crop has been destroyed by drought. Global warming will make drought more common.

◀ Huge areas of sea ice floating in the Arctic region are melting each year.

YOU CAN DO IT!

Save as much electricity as you can because making electricity produces greenhouse gases. Here are some ways you can do it:

 Turn lights off when you leave a room.

Turn down the heat. If you are cold, put on more clothes.

If something is made in a factory, ask yourself if you really need it. Only buy it if the answer is "yes."

Cars produce greenhouse gases, so use your feet! Walk or ride a bike instead of asking your parents to drive you.

READ MORE ABOUT:

• the water cycle on page 7.

Storing water

Much of the water we use comes from lakes. Where there are no natural lakes, people often make a lake by building a dam across a river. The dam controls the flow of water down the river. In rainy weather, the water collects behind the dam. The water can then be stored, cleaned and piped to farms, towns, and cities—right to your own faucet.

When a **reservoir** is made, huge areas of land are flooded. Whole villages, towns or cities may have to be moved. Thousands of square miles of rainforest have also been lost this way.

▲ Can you see trees sticking out of the water in this picture? This area used to be a forest.

▶ In 1997, work began on the Three Gorges Dam in China. It will be the largest dam ever, at 1.25 miles (2 kilometers) long and 328 feet (100 meters) tall. The reservoir it creates will be 375 miles (600 kilometers) long. It will flood two cities, 11 counties, 140 towns, 320 townships and 1,351 villages. Many river and land animals are also at risk.

Each year about 700 new dams are built in our world. Because the reservoirs contain some of the water that used to be spread out in the oceans, the planet's water balance has changed. This change makes Earth spin at a faster speed, which means that each day is about one-thousandth of a second shorter!

STOP & THINK
What will happen if we build so many dams that the rivers stop flowing?

Stopping the flow

Dams hold back the water and stop rivers from flooding. This is not always a good thing. When rivers flood, they dump rich mud, called silt, on the land. This silt makes the soil very good for growing plants. When a dam is built, the land loses this natural **fertilizer**. The silt builds up on the bottom of the dam instead.

Algae are tiny plants that can grow very fast when water is polluted with **sewage** and chemical fertilizers. They use up all the **oxygen** in the water. The algae only grows to such a thick blanket if the river does not have enough water in it to make it flow. This happens when people hold the water back with dams.

▲ The Nile River in Egypt used to flood each year. When the Aswan Dam was built, the floods stopped. Now farmers must use chemical fertilizers instead of the natural silt.

▶ This river is bright green because it is covered in a thick blanket of poisonous, slimy green algae.

YOU CAN DO IT!

- Use less water at home. Then we will not need to store so much water in reservoirs.
- Take short showers and turn off the faucet while you brush your teeth.
- Put a container outside to catch rainwater. Use this to water plants instead of using water from the faucet.
- If you live on a farm, ask your parents not to build a farm dam unless they really need to.

READ MORE ABOUT:

- polluting water with sewage on page 16
- using water and chemicals on farms on page 20.

Using water at home

If you live in a city in a **developed country**, you may think there is a never-ending supply of water. We turn on the faucet and use huge amounts in and around our homes every day.

▲ We must drink water to live. An adult needs about three-fourths of a gallon (2.5 liters) of water every day.

Things I use water for	Amount of water used
Flushing the toilet	3.5 gallons (13 liters) for a full flush
Taking a bath	32 gallons (120 liters) if bath half-full
Taking a shower	35 gallons (150 liters) for a ten-minute shower
Brushing my teeth	1.5 gallons (5 liters) with faucet running; one-fourth of a gallon (1 liter) if faucet is turned off
Washing dishes by hand	5 gallons (18 liters)
Washing dishes in a dishwasher	14.5 gallons (55 liters)
Washing clothes in a front loader	26 gallons (100 liters)
Washing clothes in a top loader	41 gallons (155 liters)
Washing the car with a hose	79 gallons (300 liters)
Running through a garden sprinkler	158 gallons (600 liters) per hour
Filling a swimming pool	5,300 to 14,500 gallons (20,000 to 55,000 liters)

STOP & THINK
Do people all over our world use the same amount of water?

The amounts are not exact. They depend on the faucets and the appliances in your home. But you can still get the idea.

Turn off the tap

There are more people in our world today than ever before. Each person in our world is using more water than ever before. Our world cannot keep supplying water at this rate. If we do not turn off the faucet, by 2025 two out of every three people in our world will not have enough water for their basic needs.

People living in cities use the most water. Modern toilets use at least 1.5 gallons (5 liters) of water each time they flush. Some people in **developing countries** have the same amount of water for all their daily needs. It is the people living in cities and in developed countries who can save the most water for our world.

80				
50				
25				
gallons per day				

City in North America / City in Australia / City in Nigeria / Village in India / Village in Kenya

▲ There is a big difference in the amount of water used around the home in different countries.

◀ In some parts of the world, people do not even have plumbing in their homes. It is a struggle to get enough water for drinking and cooking. This boy in Niger, West Africa, carries a leather bucket to fill at a well.

◀ In the United Kingdom a quarter of the water is lost because of leaky pipes. In parts of central Asia, over half the water is lost through leaky pipes.

YOU CAN DO IT!

◊ Remind your parents to fix leaky faucets.

◊ Do not take long showers. If you prefer to soak in the bath, fill it only halfway.

◊ Turn off the faucet while you brush your teeth.

◊ If you have a garden, water it early in the morning or in the evening, when less water will evaporate.

◊ If your parents have a car, use a bucket to wash it—not the hose.

READ MORE ABOUT:

• unsafe water supplies on page 25.

Wastewater down the drain

All the used water and waste from your bath, shower, sink and toilet is called sewage. In the past, sewage was emptied straight into rivers, or even onto the street in some places. In most places today, the sewage is treated. This means that the water is cleaned so that it can be returned to the water cycle.

sewage

▲ After the sewage goes down the drain, it travels into sewer pipes. The pipes take the sewage to a treatment plant where it is cleaned.

Sewage treatment

1 The sewage is passed through a screen. The screen is like a giant sieve and removes paper, plastic and grease.

2 The sewage is pumped to a settling tank. Solids sink to the bottom. These solids are called sludge. Sludge is sometimes used as a fertilizer.

3 The leftover liquid is sprayed over a bed of stones. Good **bacteria** are used to eat any waste matter that might be left.

4 The treated liquid is pumped into a river or ocean.

The good news is that in developed countries more than three-quarters of the water used in homes can go back into rivers and oceans to be recycled. The bad news is that not all of this water has been properly treated and cleaned.

STOP & THINK
What will happen if we do not treat and clean all our wastewater?

Out to sea

Untreated sewage pollutes the water and harms plant and animal life. The sewage can also end up on beaches.

It takes a lot of electricity to run a sewage treatment plant. When electricity is produced, it releases a greenhouse gas which helps trap too much heat in our world. At the same time, all this rotting sewage produces a greenhouse gas of its own, called methane. So the way we use water harms the air in our world, too.

In some places, sewage treatment ponds are now covered with heavy plastic. This traps the methane, which can be used to make electricity. Less greenhouse gas is produced this way than when electricity is made with **fossil fuels**. That solves two problems at once!

▲ It is not safe to swim in polluted water.

▲ The methane produced in these ponds can be used to make electricity.

YOU CAN DO iT!

⬦ Use a sink strainer to keep trash from being washed down the drain. Then put the scraps on the compost pile.

⬦ Do not put fat, oil or stale milk down the sink. Put them in a container in the garbage. Vegetable oil can go on the compost pile.

⬦ Do not use the toilet as a wastebasket. Put tissues, cotton swabs, plastic and other trash in the garbage.

READ MORE ABOUT:

• greenhouse gases on page 10

• using water at home on page 14.

Water for factories

In the last 150 years, factories have been used more and more to make goods for people to buy. Factories, as well as shops, restaurants, and other businesses, use water. They use water to make electricity, to mix chemicals, to wash away waste, to heat things up and to cool things down.

▲ As the number of people in our world grows, so does the number of factories. By 1980 the city of Beijing in China was using 100 times more water than it did in 1950.

▶ Look in your school bag. Water was used to make everything in there. Paper, pens, pencils, ruler, glue, lunchbox, drink bottle, raincoat—they were all made using water. Even your school bag itself was made using water.

To make this ...	it takes this amount of water ...
Chocolate bar	one-fourth gallon (1 liter)
Newspaper	2.5 gallons (9 liters)
Bicycle	34 gallons (130 liters)
Bag of cement	48 gallons (180 liters)
Car tire	50,000 gallons (190,000 liters)

STOP & THINK

What does the dirty water produced by factories do to our waterways?

Besides using a lot of precious clean water, factories produce a lot of dirty water. Much of this dirty water ends up in the sewage system or in nearby rivers. When oils, chemicals or other wastes are poured into water, they are quickly carried away and spread by the tide or by the flow of the river. They are very hard to remove.

Waterways going to waste

Pollution in waterways can poison fish and other wildlife. If hard plastic wastes are dumped into the waterways, they can choke the wildlife.

Pollution from factories is also released into the air. When this mixes with the water in clouds, it turns into **acid**. This acid falls to the ground like rain. It can kill plants and fish in lakes and rivers.

Some countries have made laws so that factories have to treat their waste before they release it into waterways. There are also laws to control the air pollution that causes acid rain.

Sometimes you cannot see pollution but it may still be there.

▲ You can see that this river is polluted.

If a lake or river gets too much acid in it, it is said to be dead. In Norway and Sweden 16,000 lakes are already dead. In Canada 14,000 lakes are dead.

Acid rain falls in lake or river and on soil.

Pollution from power stations and factories.

Acid snow on mountains.

Melting acid snow runs into soil and lake or river.

Water plants die.

Fish die.

Acid in soil is absorbed by tree roots and trees die.

▶ There are different kinds of acids. Some, such as lemon juice, are weak. Acid rain is strong. It can burn holes in your clothes.

YOU CAN DO IT!

○ Tell a parent or teacher if you think a business or factory is dumping pollution in a local waterway. They will know how to contact the local authority.

○ Buy and use less, so factories do not need to make so much. Reduce, reuse and recycle instead.

○ Ask yourself, "Do I really need this?" before you buy anything made in a factory.

READ MORE ABOUT:

• sewage treatment on page 16.

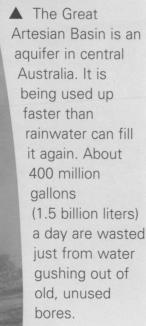

Thirsty cows and crops

Farms use up huge amounts of water. Water is used for watering crops, and livestock need water to drink. In some countries, two-thirds of the water supply is used on farms. Very little of this water is recycled.

The water that all the world's cattle, sheep, pigs, goats and chickens drink is enough to fill 120,000 big swimming pools every day.

When farmers cannot get enough water from dams or rain, they bring up water from deep underground. This groundwater has taken hundreds of thousands of years to collect in **aquifers**. If the aquifer is near the coast, the problem is even worse. If too much water is taken out, sea water seeps in and makes the water salty.

Most farmers use chemicals on their farms to make crops grow and to keep insects from eating them. These chemicals can run off into waterways or move down into underground water.

▲ The Great Artesian Basin is an aquifer in central Australia. It is being used up faster than rainwater can fill it again. About 400 million gallons (1.5 billion liters) a day are wasted just from water gushing out of old, unused bores.

▶ Farm chemicals can find their way into the water.

STOP & THINK

Are there ways to farm without using harmful chemicals and so much water?

Smart farming

The good news is that scientists are teaching farmers new ways to grow crops without using so much water. Farmers used to always remove the stones from their fields. Now scientists think it is good to leave the stones. Stones create cool spots to shelter new plants. Scientists are also telling farmers to plant trees. Tree roots hold water in the soil. They provide shade so that crops need less water.

Some farmers grow food without using harmful chemicals. This is called organic farming. The fruit may not look as good as fruit grown with chemicals, but it is better for you and for our world—and it often tastes better!

▲ These farmers in Colombia are replanting trees in an area that was cleared by logging.

YOU CAN DO iT!

○ Write to local water and sewage authorities and suggest they use treated sewage for watering farms instead of letting it go into rivers.

○ Eat less meat. In some parts of the world, to get a certain amount of beef you need to feed the cow seven times this amount of grain. This means you have used water to grow the grain and to raise the cow. You would get more food and use less water if you just ate the grain yourself!

From drains to waterways

The next time it rains, watch what happens to the rain that falls on the paths and road outside your house. In natural environments most of the rain soaks into the ground. When there are a lot of hard surfaces, such as roads and roofs, the rain cannot soak into the ground. Gutters channel the excess rainwater into drains, which carry it to local waterways. This is called stormwater.

Stormwater picks up a lot of pollution and garbage on its way to the drains. Unlike sewage that is treated and cleaned, stormwater flows straight into the waterways.

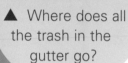

▲ Where does all the trash in the gutter go?

Stormwater can carry

- oil, grease and rubber from roads
- fertilizers and pesticides from farms and gardens
- animal droppings
- paint and oil poured down drains
- chemicals dumped from factories
- soil, leaves and trash dumped in gutters
- detergents from washing the car.

One can of paint poured onto the ground near your house can pollute 250,000 times that amount of water.

Waterway pollutants do not always come from drains. Poisonous wastes and sewage have been dumped into waterways from special dump ships. Sometimes ships or oil rigs spill oil into the ocean.

STOP & THINK

How much more garbage can the oceans take?

▶ One of the most well known disasters happened in 1989. The tanker *Exxon Valdez* struck a reef off Prince William Sound in Alaska. About 13 million gallons (50 million liters) of oil spilled out and spread along the coast. About 250,000 birds and thousands of marine mammals were killed.

Oceans of garbage

Human-made pollution that does not break down in nature is the most dangerous. Trees drop millions of leaves every year, but leaves are biodegradable. This means they rot and go slowly into the soil. Many chemicals and plastics are not biodegradable. When they get into the water, they stay there and poison it.

More than half of the garbage entering our world's oceans each year is plastic. This plastic can choke the birds and sea life and spoil recreation areas such as beaches. Litter traps can stop some of this garbage from entering waterways, but it is better not to dump it in the first place.

▲ Most of this trash is not biodegradable.

International laws have been made to try and stop dumping, but it sometimes still happens. Some companies now try to produce packaging that is biodegradable or that can be reused.

◀ In some places, litter traps have been put in to try and stop the trash from moving into rivers or oceans.

YOU CAN DO IT!

◊ Use fewer chemical detergents and cleaners. Read the labels on cleaners before you buy them to see if the cleaners are "environmentally friendly" or biodegradable.

◊ If your parents own a car, wash it on the grass instead of the road or driveway. The detergent will fertilize the grass!

◊ Pick up litter so it does not end up in stormwater.

READ MORE ABOUT:

• sewage and other wastewater on pages 16 and 19.

Dissolving— good and bad

Water is vital to all living things. It is so useful because chemicals easily **dissolve** in it. Plants can take in food through their roots because the food is dissolved in water. And it is the water inside animals that helps them to absorb the food and oxygen they need to live.

The very thing that makes water so important also makes water very easy to pollute. In addition to food and oxygen, chemicals and poisons dissolve in water. The chemicals and poisons can then enter the water cycle at any point and be carried through the environment, doing damage.

Even underground water in aquifers is getting more polluted with factory wastewater, sewage, farm chemicals and salty water. Once the water in aquifers is polluted, it is almost impossible to clean up.

▲ All living things need water to survive.

▶ The aquifer under Bangkok is polluted with factory waste and human sewage.

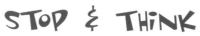

STOP & THINK
What happens if people drink polluted water?

24

Drinking unsafe water

About 10 million people die every year from diseases carried in dirty drinking water. About 80 percent of all sicknesses in our world are caused by unsafe water supplies.

In many parts of the world, especially in developing countries, people get sick and die because the water they drink is dirty and contains bacteria. When there is no clean water to drink, people have to drink the dirty water or die of thirst.

Our world is full of food chains. Small animals are eaten by bigger animals, which in turn are eaten by even bigger animals. The poisonous chemicals that are in tiny amounts at the bottom of the chain collect as they move up the chain. So the animals at the top of the chain—such as people—get the biggest dose of poison.

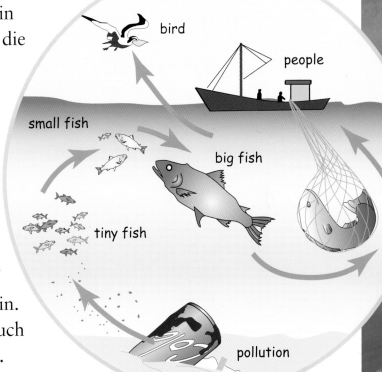

bird

people

small fish

big fish

tiny fish

pollution

▶ The animal at the top of the chain has much more of the poison in its body than the animal at the bottom.

YOU CAN DO iT!

- Do not drop litter.
- Use fewer chemical detergents and cleaners. Soap gets water dirty, not clean.
- Reuse plastic bags as many times as possible.
- Recycle as much as you can. If there is less waste to deal with overall, we will have more time to work out ways of dealing with dangerous waste.

READ MORE ABOUT:

- the water cycle on page 7
- pollution of underground water on page 20.

OUR WORLD

Salty water

Most water comes from our world's four salty oceans. Find out how this water gets into the air and how the salt is left behind.

What you need:

- 2 pints (1 liter) of water
- shallow pan
- 3 tablespoons of salt.

What to do:

1. Pour the water into the pan.

2. Make sea water by adding the salt to the water and stirring until it dissolves.

3. Leave the pan in a sunny spot.

What happens?

The sun's heat evaporates the water. The salt, which is a solid, is left behind. The same thing happens when water evaporates from the ocean. Just imagine if it did not—rain would be salty!

Sweating keeps you cool

Water in the oceans helps control the heat in our world. It is the same with your own body. When you are hot, sweat comes out of tiny pores in your skin. The heat from your body then changes the sweat from a liquid to water vapor. The sweat evaporates and goes into the air to join the water cycle.

Prove it!

Blow on the top of your hand. Remember how cool or warm it felt. Now lick the top of your hand. Imagine that this is sweat. Blow on your wet hand. Your skin will feel much cooler this time. Blowing on your wet hand made the water evaporate. Evaporation needs heat. It took the heat from your hand, so your hand felt cool.

Sandy filter

Water has to be stored, treated and cleaned before it can be piped to your home. Make this water filter. It will show you one way that water can be cleaned. It is much simpler than the filters at a water treatment plant.

What you need:

- adult helper
- large plastic drink bottle, empty and clean
- scissors
- clean sand
- pan
- soapy water.

What to do:

1. Ask the adult helper to cut off the top third of the bottle and make a few holes in the bottom.

2. Fill half the bottle with sand.

3. Hold the bottle over the pan. Pour soapy water on the sand.

What happens?

Water will drip out the bottom of the bottle. It will not be as soapy as the water you poured in. The sand filters soap from the water.

Water report

If you live near a river or beach, look out for signs of pollution. If you see any of the things in the pictures on this page, you know you are looking at polluted water. Take a sniff. Even if the water looks clean, your nose will often tell you if it is polluted.

▲ Green algae

▼ Garbage

Do not drink the water from your filter. It might still be dirty.

Think globally

Everything in our world is connected. Look at the map of our world. The four oceans all flow into each other. Whatever we do to water in one part of our world affects the water cycle for our whole world. The oceans are not just one country's responsibility. All countries need to work together to save water and to keep it clean.

Working together

Some rivers flow through more than one country. The Rhine River runs through Switzerland, France, Germany and the Netherlands (Holland). In the 1970s, it was so polluted that fish died and people could not use its water for drinking. The four countries worked together to clean it up. Today most chemical and sewage discharges into the river have been stopped. The fish are back and the water can again be used for drinking.

▲ The oceans are very big, but this does not mean we should pollute them.

▶ The Rhine River has been cleaned up because of cooperation between countries.

STOP & THINK
What will happen if all countries do not use water wisely and share water fairly?

Governments in action

There is only a limited amount of fresh water in our world, and it is not spread evenly across the planet. All countries must think about the impact of using water from rivers that they share with other countries.

Sharing water	
Middle East	Israel shares the Jordan River and aquifers with its Arab neighbors
North Africa	Egypt and eight other countries share the Nile River
South Asia	India, Bangladesh and Pakistan share 140 rivers

In 1992 governments from around the world, met at an Earth Summit in Brazil. It was the world's biggest meeting. All the leaders at the meeting signed an agreement called Agenda 21. It is a plan for using—and looking after—our world in the 21st century. All countries could do more to keep our world healthy. The strength of Agenda 21 is that the world's leaders agreed that we need to take action.

▲ These children were part of the Earth Summit in Brazil in 1992.

Agenda 21: Aims for our water

- Share fresh water **resources** fairly.
- Provide clean water for everyone.
- Stop wasting water.
- Stop polluting water.

YOU CAN DO iT!

◊ Talk to your parents about ways to use less water and to create less water pollution.

◊ Help to clean up a local river or beach.

◊ Tell the local authority if you see river or beach pollution.

◊ Join an environmental group that is campaigning for cleaner rivers and oceans.

◊ Write to politicians and tell them what you think needs to be done to keep rivers clean.

Sustaining our world

To survive on this planet, we need to take and use the things our world gives us. But we also need to keep all the parts of our world working in balance. Scientists call it ecologically sustainable development. It means taking only what we need from our world to live today, and at the same time keeping our world healthy so it can keep giving in the future.

If you add the water used in farming and in industry to the water used in homes, people use six times more water today than they did in 1950. The water supply is not endless. As the population grows, we need to save water to make sure everyone has their share—today and tomorrow.

Everything in our world is connected. If we damage one part, we can affect the other parts. And if we look after one part, we can help protect all the other parts. The future of our world depends on our actions now.

▼ The different parts of our world are all connected.

Glossary

acid a chemical that eats away solid material

aquifers deep underground layers of rock containing water

atmosphere the thin layer of gases that surrounds Earth

bacteria tiny organisms that live in soil, water, plants, animals and people

developed country a country where the way of life is based on the use of resources by industries

developing countries countries based on farming that are trying to develop their resources

dissolve completely mix into another substance

evaporates changes from a liquid into a gas. For example, if you boil water (liquid) it changes into water vapor (gas)

fertilizer something added to the soil to make plants grow faster or bigger

fossil fuels fuels such as coal or gas that formed in Earth from the remains of animals and plants

glaciers large, slow-moving masses of ice

greenhouse effect the trapping of the sun's heat close to Earth

oxygen the gas in the air that all plants and animals need to live

reservoir a lake that forms behind a dam

resources things that people make use of

sewage waste carried away in the sewers and drains

Index